DATE DUE			

In My Neighborhood

POSTAL WORKERS

With thanks to Deby Martin

P. B. and K. L.

First U.S. edition 1999

Text copyright © 1992 by Paulette Bourgeois
Illustrations copyright © 1992 by Kim LaFave

Published in Canada by   Published in the U.S. by
Kids Can Press Ltd.   Kids Can Press Ltd.
29 Birch Avenue   4500 Witmer Industrial Estates
Toronto, ON, M4V 1E2   Niagara Falls, NY 14305-1386

US   99 0 9 8 7 6 5 4 3 2 1
US PA   00 0 9 8 7 6 5 4 3 2 1

Designed by N.R. Jackson
Typeset by Cybergraphics Co. Inc.
Printed in Hong Kong by Sheck Wah Tong
Printing Press Limited

Canadian Cataloguing in Publication Data

Bourgeois, Paulette
   Postal workers

(In my neighborhood)
ISBN 1-55074-504-2 (bound) ISBN 1-55074-785-1 (pbk.)

1. Postal service — Employees — Juvenile literature.
2. Postal service — Juvenile literature. I. LaFave, Kim.
II. Series: Bourgeois, Paulette. In my neighborhood.

HE6371.B68 2000   j383.4   C98-931965-2

Kids Can Press is a Nelvana company

In My Neighborhood

POSTAL WORKERS

Paulette Bourgeois

Kim LaFave

KIDS CAN PRESS

"Oh, no!" says Gordon. "Grandma's birthday
is only five days away and I haven't sent a card."

Gordon chooses his very best paper and
draws a picture of rainbows and balloons. He
writes a special message and puts the card in
an envelope.

He crosses his fingers. "I hope she gets
this in time."

The card must travel all the way
across the country.

Gordon writes Grandma's address and his address on the front of the
envelope. He checks the zip code twice — mail moves faster when
the address is correct. Then he walks to the post office to buy a stamp.

The money for the stamp pays for the mail to travel from one place to another. When people send special mail, such as big parcels or rush mail, they pay more money to the post office for the extra service.

Gordon looks at all the stamps and chooses very carefully. He licks the glue on the back of the stamp and sticks it on before he slides his card into the mailbox.

Letters and small packages are dropped into a local mailbox. Every day, sometimes two or three times a day, the mail is collected by a mail carrier and taken to the local post office so that the mail can be sorted by destination.

All of the letters and packages that are collected are then sent to a processing center, sorted further, and put into a sack with others going to the same area. Most sorting is done by machine. Postal workers sort out special mail, parcels and letters that are too big or too small for the machines.

A machine called an advance-facer-canceler does three jobs in one. Just in case the human sorters missed an odd-sized envelope, the machine spits out all the mail that won't fit. Then it makes sure that all the fronts of the envelopes are facing the same direction.

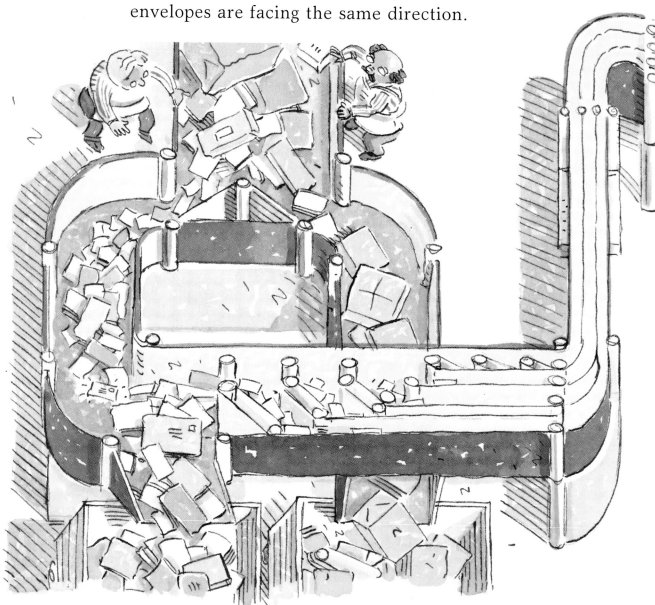

Next, the machine cancels the stamps by making a squiggly mark on them. A canceled stamp cannot be used again. Stamps are like tickets — they're good for only one trip!

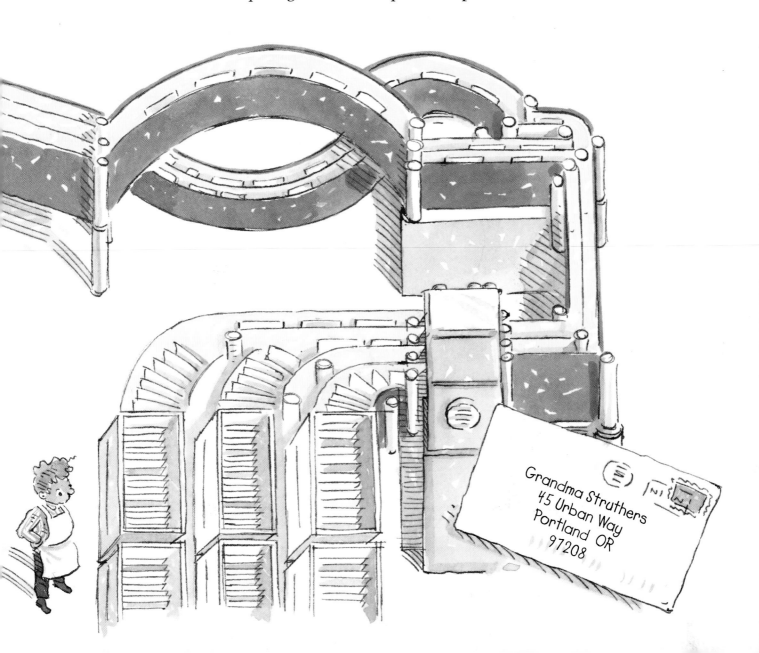

Grandma Struthers
45 Urban Way
Portland OR
97208

Every address in the United States has a zip code made up of five numbers. Most five-digit zip codes also have a four-digit "add on" code. A postal worker can tell almost exactly where you live, just by reading your zip code! If your zip code is 53404, you live in Wisconsin; 95476 is northern California; the President of the United States has a zip code, too! It is 20036, or Washington, D.C. Gordon's grandmother lives in Portland, Oregon. Her zip code is 97208.

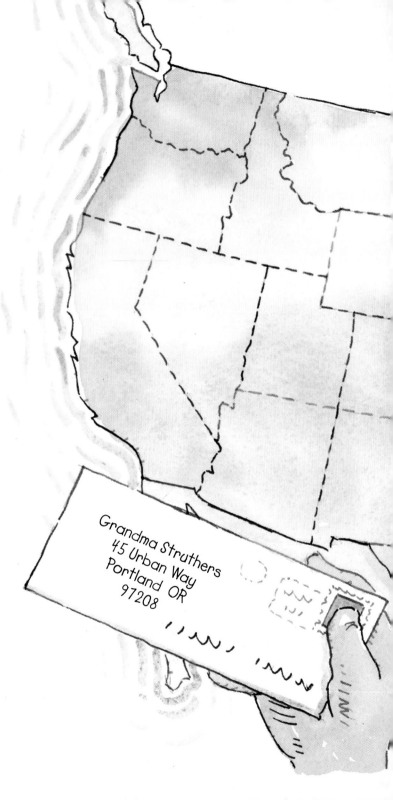

Grandma Struthers
45 Urban Way
Portland OR
97208

Most letter sorting in a post office is done by machine. An operator reads the address on a letter and punches a keyboard that prints a code of dots and bars. Other sorting machines "read" the codes and sort letters further.

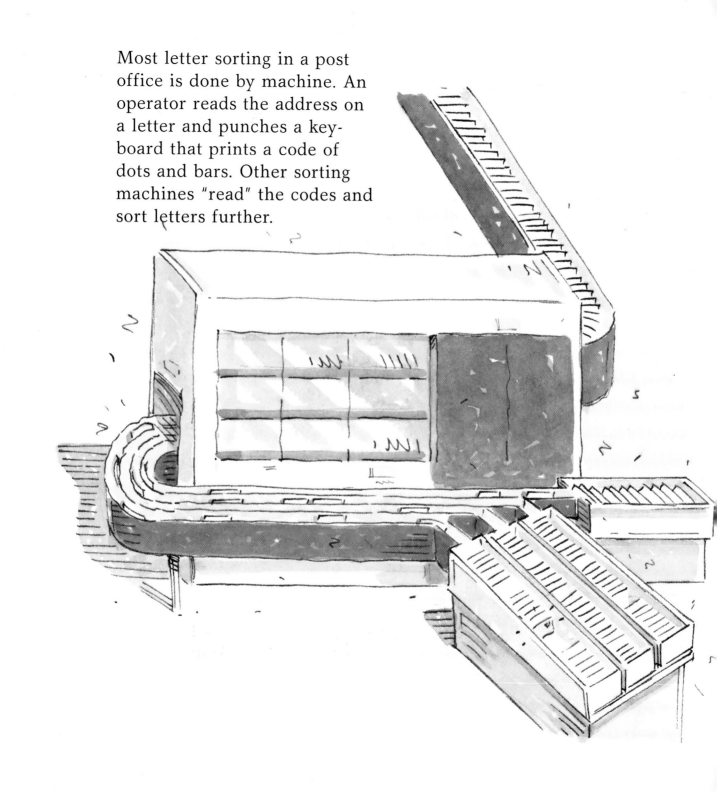

Letters whiz through a sorting machine that reads the computerized zip codes and sorts the envelopes onto different conveyor belts. Gordon's letter moves along the belt until it drops into a bag marked Portland. The mail bags travel mostly by truck and by plane.

The card from Gordon has traveled night and day to the postal station near his Grandma's.

It is still cold, dark and early when Grandma's letter carrier gets to work. A postal worker has already sorted the mail into routes and put it into big, heavy bags.

The letter carrier picks up her satchel and sorts her mail into slots that are marked by street and building numbers. "Whew!" she says. "Must be a lot of birthdays coming up."

There's too much mail for the letter carrier to take all at once. She puts as much mail as she can carry into her satchel. The rest she puts into bags that will be taken by a driver to locked corner boxes on her route. The letter carriers drag their bags to the waiting trucks. "Hurry, hurry," the drivers shout.

Letter carriers have to be ready for snow, sleet, sun, rain.

Full bags can weigh up to 35 pounds (16 kilograms) eac

Dark running shoes or boots

Needs new shoes every couple of months

SPRING

SUMMER

Shoulder flashes on
each arm

Must be physically fit

AUTUMN

WINTER

The letter carrier walks fast on her route. She steps around garbage cans, marches up steps and slides the mail into mail slots. She watches out for ice in the winter. And she hopes owners of angry dogs will keep them leashed and out of her way.

Letter carriers deliver the mail; they do not read it — not even funny postcards from far away. But they do care who collects their mail and who doesn't. Some postal workers are community watchdogs. They know the elderly people on their route.

When their mail is not collected, the postal worker calls a special phone number to report something suspicious. Perhaps the person fell and can't get up. A relative or friend is sent to check. Postal workers save lives this way.

By the time the letter carrier reaches her corner box, called a relay box, her satchel is empty. She uses a key to spring the lock open. She fills her shoulder bag again. "What a gorgeous yellow envelope," she says.

Grandma gets a big smile on her face when she opens her mailbox. There are cards from all over the world. "Goodness, something from Gordon. His card is early. My birthday isn't until tomorrow."

Grandma tapes Gordon's card on her fridge. She loves the card, but she loves the stamp on the envelope, too. Grandma is a stamp collector. She takes out a large leather binder and adds Gordon's birthday stamp to her collection.

On her other mail, there are stamps from Canada, Japan, Peru and Greece. She already knows what she will send Gordon for his birthday: a card made of special paper with a dozen stamps from a dozen countries tucked inside an envelope.

Grandma seals her envelope
and addresses it carefully.

She puts the stamp here.

She puts her address on the top left corner
of the envelope like this:

MRS. A. STRUTHERS
45 URBAN WAY
PORTLAND OR
97208

She puts Gordon's address in the center of
the envelope like this: GORDON NORMAN
2 CORTLAND RD
ENDICOTT NY
13761

Gordon checks his community mailbox every day. Soon it will be his birthday, and Grandma always sends him a big fat envelope with something special tucked inside.